The Easy Guide to Wicca for Beginners

2 Books in 1 - Learn Wiccan Traditions, Eclectic Witches, Solitary Practitioners, Candle Magic, and Protection Spells

By Frank Bawdoe

Table of Contents

YOUR FREE GIFT!

Thank you for adding this book to your Wiccan Library! To learn more, join Frank's Wiccan Community and get this additional free **Little Book of Magic Spells 100% FREE!**

Little Book of Magic Spells is a great starting point for beginners looking to try their hand at practicing magic spells. It includes **19 beginner-friendly spells** that can help you create a positive atmosphere within your home, protect yourself from negativity, improve your overall health, attract love and prosperity. Hundreds of others are already enjoying insider access to all of my current and future full-length books, 100% free!

If you want insider access plus this **free Little Book of Magic Spells,** all you have to do is **scan the code below** with your smartphone camera to claim your offer!

SPECIAL BONUS!

Thank you for adding this book to your Wiccan Library! To learn more, join Frank's Wiccan Community and get this additional free *Wicca Starter Kit* book 100% FREE!

Hundreds of others are already enjoying insider access to all of my current and future full-length books, **100% free!**

If you want insider access plus this free *Wicca Starter Kit* book, all you have to do is **scan the code below** to claim your offer!

Book 1: Wicca Starter Kit for Beginners

"I remember writing the series with great enthusiasm, and I hope this enthusiasm continues to inspire newcomers to see the truly life-changing possibilities Wicca can offer. As a 'religion of self-expression,' I wish everyone an inspiring quest on this path called Wicca." — Morgana Sythove

There is a reason why more and more people gravitate towards Wicca, so what makes this magical religion so special?

Witches have been a huge part of pop culture with TV shows like Bewitched, Merlin, and Sabrina, the Teenage Witch. This has resulted in people's growing interest in Wicca. Although people of all ages and genders find this religion appealing, young women in specific have been showing interest in learning about it. This is mainly because they find something relatable in this religion with the Goddesses and the idea of a female divine; these strong and powerful deities inspire young women. Additionally, since many people are now concerned with the environment, they find comfort in Wicca, glorifying nature.

Whatever your reasons are for learning about Wicca, we provide all of the vital information you will need to get started in this book. We will discuss Wicca covens, where witches meet to worship and practice magic to connect with the spirit world. As a beginner, it is essential to know all about the different Wiccan practices, including contemporary practices, that will guide you into understanding neo-paganism. In this book, we also discuss solitary practice, which is where Wiccans opt out of joining a coven to practice magic solo.

There are also various Wicca traditions. Some are traditional, while others are more eclectic. Eclectic Wicca traditions also fall under the Neo-Wiccan category. Many coven and solitary Wiccans follow these modernized traditions and apply the name to various unique practices and modified traditions which are discussed in detail in this book. Additionally, we also cover in-depth the different types of covens and circles and the pros and cons of covens. This information will help you choose between joining a coven or becoming a solo practitioner. We end the book by giving you additional information to help you find your Wiccan path.

You should learn everything about the Wicca religion, including all of the different ways you can practice it, which will make the transition to your new belief much easier. When we decided we wanted to practice Wicca, we were looking for a guide to get us started. Now that we have done our research and become a Wicca practitioner, we have decided to help others who are struggling to find their path as we were by providing all of the information they will need in one place. Our research was thorough, we read various books and articles about the subject, and we also spoke with a few Wicca practitioners to help us write the type of book that you will need at this stage. The more we learn and read about Wicca, the more we fall in love with this religion.

Many people want to learn about Wicca, whether out of curiosity or to practice an independent religion free from formal institutional structure. Here, we made sure to provide everything you need to know about Wicca. You may be just starting out, but with every page, you will learn something new and gain the kind of experience and awareness about the fascinating religion of Wicca that would otherwise take months or years of research on your part. Now let's begin your journey by navigating the world of Wicca traditions: the ancient pagan and modern ones. To echo the sentiments of the quote we mentioned above, we hope this book becomes an inspiration to all Wicca beginners.

Chapter 1: What Are the Most Popular Wiccan Traditions?

"Witchcraft is, and was, not... for everyone. Unless you have an attraction to the occult, a sense of wonder, a feeling that you can slip for a few minutes out of the world into the world of faery, it is of no use to you." - Gerald Gardner

The Ancient and Neo-Pagan Traditions of Wicca

Wicca is a modern religion with ancient traditions. In this chapter, we discuss all Wicca traditions, from the ones derived from ancient traditions to neo-pagan ones. We have selected some of the most popular traditions to better understand your new religion.

The Gardnerian Tradition

The Gardnerian Wicca tradition was founded by Gerrald B. Gardner, who is named after. Gardner was a part of the New Forest Coven. He used some of their beliefs and the practices of Kabbalah, ceremonial magic, and various other sources to create the Gardnerian tradition. Gardner then started initiating a high priestess who initiated other members into the coven. This was one of the main things that helped the Wicca religion grow in the United Kingdom. One of the people initiated into Gardner's coven was Buckland Raymond, who helped spread this Wiccan tradition in America. In many ways, the Gardnerian path is considered the first Wiccan tradition, with some people arguing that it is the only true tradition.

The main focus of the Gardnerian tradition is the worship of the Horned God (the God of magic, death, and hunting) and the Great Goddess (who is usually incarnated as a Maiden or a Great Mother). Its main beliefs are that death is inevitable, reincarnations are part of the cycle of life, and life is valuable. This neo-pagan tradition also honors nature, celebrates the eight Sabbats, and believes in the individual's freedom as long as they don't cause harm to anyone.

The Gardnerians used to prefer to perform their rituals naked because they believed that nudity makes them equals and brings them closer to nature. However, nowadays, many covens prefer to wear robes and have forsaken nudity. All rituals take place inside a magic circle created using traditional rules. Privacy is key when it comes to these circles. These covens don't believe in practicing any dark magic or evil spells; they only focus on healing and positive magic.

The Alexandrian Tradition

The Alexandrian Wicca Tradition was founded by Alex Sanders and his wife, Maxine. Before forming his own coven and tradition, Sanders was a member of one of the Gardnerian covens, which is why you will find many similarities between the two. However, the Alexandrian tradition gives their deities names and uses ritual tools that differ from the Gardnerian. This tradition, which is hugely influenced by Gardnerian tradition, combines various ceremonial magic and Hermetic Kabbalah. You will find that people usually practice in different ways, which is the case with many magical lores.

This tradition gives value to both genders, which is why they dedicate the same amount of time to the Goddess and the God during ceremonies and rites. The covens mainly focus on ceremonial magic, and their meetings take place on a full moon, new moon, and during the eight Wiccan Sabbats. Additionally, they only allow priests and priestesses because they are the only ones who can communicate with the Divine.

Just like the Gardnerian tradition, the Alexandrian coven uses a degree system to initiate its members. In some covens, some members are initiated into beginner levels and then advance, while in other covens, they are given First Degree titles right away. According to the Alexandrian tradition, a priest must initiate a priestess and vice versa. Nowadays, it has become almost impossible to tell the difference between these two traditions, which is why each coven accepts degreed members from the other.

The Dianic Tradition

The Dianic Wicca tradition was founded by the witch Zsuzsanna Budapest. This tradition was hugely influenced by the feminist movement, which is why its members place more attention on the Goddess rather than the God. The majority of the Dianic tradition are women, but some covens have started welcoming a few men for the sake of polarity. Although Dianic Wiccan means "lesbian witch," the covens accept women of all sexual orientations.

We mentioned that many traditions only practice positive magic. However, this isn't the case with the Dianic tradition. Since it is influenced by feminism and Zsuzsanna Budapest is a feminist herself, she believes that it is acceptable to use binding or hexing against anyone who harms women. In fact, she has called on various occasions for any man who commits sexual violence against a woman or a child to be hexed.

That said, they still share similarities with other traditions. For instance, the covens use similar altar tools and celebrate the eight Sabbats. You won't find many practices or rituals within the Dianic tradition. They merely follow a Goddess and focus on feminine spirituality.

Seax-Wicca Tradition

The Seax-Wicca tradition was founded by Raymond Buckland, one of the prominent figures in Wicca history. This tradition mainly focuses on the Germanic deities of Freya, Woden, and other entities as well. The practices of the Seax-Wicca lore are hugely influenced by the Nordic Runes, which is the Viking alphabet. This alphabet is associated with magic and modern divination.

This tradition is different from the Gardnerian and other traditions as they are open and don't use a secret oath. However, their books may give off the impression that they are more of a secret coven, but this isn't the case. For instance, Buckland doesn't give much information in his book "Buckland's Book of Saxon Witchcraft" about the tools used in ritual circles. This has nothing to do with privacy, but he probably assumed that every practitioner already knows this.

The Seax-Wicca covens don't only perform initiations but also welcome solitary witches and self-initiation. This has given a new generation of solitary practitioners a chance to partake in this folklore. Unlike other covens, the Seax-Wicca tradition is more democratic as they elect their officers and can impeach them if necessary. There are usually four officers in a Seax-Wicca coven: the High Priestess, the High Priest, the Scribe, and the Thegn. The Thegn is the person who takes care of the meeting area in the coven, protects it, and prepares it for magical rituals. Democracy and the fact that solitary practitioners are embraced have made many people gravitate toward this belief.

Although there is a significant difference between the Seax-Wicca tradition and the ones we have mentioned in this chapter, it still shares some similarities. In fact, Buckland was influenced by both the Gardnerian and Alexandrian traditions when he created the Seax-Wicca tradition. Buckland wanted to avoid any confusion between his tradition and pre-Christian Saxon custom. Although the Goddess and God, Freya, and Woden, are Anglo-Saxon deities, he gave Celtic names to the Wiccan holidays, which the practitioners can relate to.

Buckland had a different approach to practicing Wicca as he didn't see magic as merely practicing spells and rituals but as an energy that can adjust itself to modern times.

Celtic Wicca Traditions

We should note here that Celtic Wicca and Celtic paganism aren't the same, although they do share many similarities. They differ because Celtic Paganism is an ancient belief while Wicca is a modern religion. So why do people confuse the two? This is mainly because Gardner was heavily influenced by Celtic lore when he created his Wiccan tradition and ideology.

Celtic Gods Worshipped by the Celtic Wiccans

The Goddess Rosmerta

Rosmerta means the great provider, and she is the Goddess of prosperity and healing. Wiccans call on this Goddess when they need help with material things like financial guidance or employment.

The Goddess Brigid

Brigid is the Goddess of crafts, poetry, and healing. She represents fertility and the arrival of spring. She is one of the most popular Celtic Wiccan Goddesses, as they see her as the Goddess of new growth and spring. She is celebrated on the first and second of February in a festival named after her. Wiccans believe Brigid provides healing, wisdom, divination, inspiration, abundance, and peace. She also represents women's power, compassion, and love.

The Goddess Rhiannon

Rhiannon is the Goddess of the moon. Wiccans seek her guidance when they find themselves the victims in a situation or want the truth to be revealed. She represents forgiveness and patience and is called on during magical rituals that have to do with self-confidence and divination.

The God Lugh

Lugh is the God of artisans, smiths, and harvests. When Wiccans need inspiration for any creative matters, this is who they turn to.

The God Cernunnos

Cernunnos is the horned God of hunting who we mentioned earlier. He represents masculine energy and fertility and is a very important God in the Wicca religion. According to Wiccans, he represents one side of the dualistic universe. He is also a symbol of death and the night.

The Goddess Cerridwen

Cerridwen is the Goddess of prophecy and transformation. According to Wiccans, transformation, change, and rebirth are all representative of her. Embodying many archetypes, Cerridwen is also known as a Triple Goddess.

Faery Wicca

Faery, unlike the supernatural creature fairy, is a spirit deity. This branch of Wicca is about worshipping the deities of ancient Celts. However, these deities are faces or other supernatural creatures. They are incorporated into magical practices that celebrate certain pagan holidays like lunar, seasonal, and solar cycles, the Divine, nature, and Earth's rhythms. The practitioners of Faery Wicca can either join a coven or become solitary practitioners.

This religion can have a huge impact on enriching your existence and daily experiences. Most of its practices and rituals take place in nature like groves, forests, or near any body of water. However, if being around nature isn't possible, you can use any natural elements in your spells and rituals.

Inside the covens, you will find initiators and elder priests or priestesses. However, if you don't want to join a coven, you can still pursue the Faery Wicca and reach the highest levels of knowledge alone.

First, to practice Faery Wicca, learn about ancient methodology, traditions, and lore. Familiarizing yourself with the Faeries will make connecting to them a lot easier. You can achieve this connection through meditation or visualization. When you master that part, you will be able to use spells and rituals to connect with spirits.

Norse Wicca

The last Wiccan belief on this list is Norse Wicca, which is based on pre-Christianity Scandinavian beliefs, as made clear from the name. Practitioners of this religion worship various deities who tend to have human qualities. They have personalities, feelings, flaws, talents; they fall in love, fight, get married, and have kids. The believers see the divine in everything around them, including nature, animals, and objects.

In this chapter, we have discussed:

- The Gardnerian Wicca tradition, which is the first tradition and, as some argue, the only true tradition

- The Alexandrian tradition which is quite similar to the Gardnerian tradition but focuses on deities of both genders

- The Dianic tradition, which was created as a result of the feminism movement

- The Seax-Wicca tradition differs from the others since it focuses on electing coven officers

- The Celtic Wicca and the deities they worshiped

- The Faery Wicca focuses on worshipping supernatural entities

- Norse Wicca and their unique Gods

There are many traditions within the Wicca religion, each with an interesting history. Many of them share some similarities, but you will also find that each one has its unique qualities and a different approach. Whether you are a feminist looking for a coven related to your interests, find yourself gravitating towards a more democratic coven, or want to become a solitary practitioner, you will definitely find a tradition that will appeal to you on this list. Now that you know the most popular Wiccan traditions and how they are practiced, we move on to the next chapter to familiarize you with the subject of Eclectic Wicca.

Chapter 2: What Is Eclectic Wicca?

"Spiritual practice isn't about getting anything; it's about uncovering." - Elizabeth Lesser

According to the dictionary, the term eclectic means obtaining ideas, taste, or style from a diverse and wide range of sources. The Merriam Dictionary also defines the word as the act of choosing what seems to be the best from numerous styles, doctrines, or methods. As you may have already guessed, this is exactly what eclectic Wiccans and Pagans do. They often practice their beliefs on their own or join formal or informal groups that share their convictions.

What Makes an Eclectic Wiccan?

There are numerous reasons why an individual or coven may perceive themselves as eclectic. These reasons include:

- **Practicing Mixed and Matched Traditions**: The coven or person may adopt a blend of practices, spiritual activities, and beliefs derived from various distinct traditions and pantheons.

- **Practicing Modified Traditions:** A set of Wiccans may establish a group that is a spinoff of an existing Wiccan tradition, like Gardnerian and Alexandrian. However, this version includes modification and variation that makes it significantly different from the initial tradition.

- **Practicing Personalized Methods:** Many Wiccans prefer to create their own versions of beliefs, traditions, and practices. Their experience is unique, which is why it falls under the umbrella of eclectic Wicca.

- **Practicing without Being Initiated**: Those who had to explore the Wiccan belief system on their own and learn the tradition from the internet, or other publicly available resources, are often considered eclectic Wiccans. This is because they likely didn't use oathbound or other initiatory material.

NeoWicca

There is often a lot of disagreement and controversy when it comes to determining who truly is Wiccan and who isn't. This is usually because there is a lot of confusion surrounding Wiccan traditions that have existed for centuries and newer eclectic ones. Many people suggest that only lineage traditions and their practitioners should be allowed to consider themselves Wiccan. In that sense, anyone who believed themselves to be eclectic is therefore NeoWiccan, and not Wiccan. It is worth highlighting that being a NeoWiccan is not a derogatory label, nor does it mean that you're less of a Wiccan than others who follow lineage Wiccan traditions. It simply means that you practice and follow newer, yet just as relevant, forms of Wicca.

The Church of Universal Eclectic Wicca

The Church of Universal Eclectic Wicca is one of the organizations in support of eclectic Wiccans. The church defines universalism as a spiritual belief system that allows people to search for and find the truth in numerous places. Eclecticism, in that sense, is the practice of deriving this information from various places. Hence, the organization is named the Church of Universal Eclectic Wicca.

This church encourages its followers to explore their spirituality and experiment with different practices. It urges you to determine what works for you in terms of religion and spirituality and let go of the things that don't resonate with you. This organization views Wicca as any spiritual system that claims to be Wicca. It believes in the existence of a force, God, power, or anything that manifests as both genders and is genderless.

The Church of Universal Eclectic Wicca also goes by the Five Points of Wiccan Belief. These are the Wiccan Rede, the Law of Return, the Ethic of Self-Responsibility, the Ethic of Constant Improvement, and the Ethic of Attunement. The Wiccan Rede can be written in numerous ways. However, the core message remains consistent: to do whatever you desire as long as you don't harm anyone. The Law of Return suggests that the energy a person manifests into the world, whether positive or negative, will return to them threefold.

Solitary Practice

Many NeoWiccans and Pagans prefer to practice alone rather than join a group. There are various reasons why someone would prefer to practice alone. Perhaps they work better, feel a deeper connection when no one else is around, or there are no nearby covens to join.

Many people can't imagine practicing as a solitary. Others, however, wouldn't want to do it any other way. Both methods of practicing have their pros and cons. Fortunately, you can always change your mind and test out a different way if one isn't suitable for you. One of the main benefits that solitary practitioners enjoy is following their own schedules. When they are not bound to a certain group, they don't have to think about building relationships with other coven members. Most importantly, solitary practitioners can work at their own pace. The cons, however, include the need for guidance and a human source of knowledge.

There are a few things you need to take into consideration if you wish to practice Eclectic Wicca in solitary, including the following:

You Need a Daily Routine

There's nothing harder than maintaining consistency when you decide to take on a task with no one to answer to. This applies to almost every aspect of your life. For instance, if you go to the gym with a friend, you are less likely to procrastinate or skip your workout session than you would if you go by yourself or work out at home. Therefore, you need to develop a solid daily routine that allows you to stay on top of your tasks. This could include reading up on your tradition, meditating, or doing ritual work. Make sure to schedule at least one task a day to work toward reaching your spiritual goals.

Keep a Spiritual Diary

Many people like to keep a BoS (Book of Shadows), a rituals journal, or a magical chronicle to keep spiritual information or record certain experiences. Taking notes throughout your journey is very important for several reasons. For example, this allows you to keep a record of things you've experimented with. It also lets you keep track of the things that work for you and what things don't. Writing down spellwork, prayers, and rituals allows you to build a foundation for your practices and tradition, especially if you're an eclectic practitioner. As we mentioned, an aspect of eclectic Wicca is determining what works for you and incorporating them into your practice. This makes it a highly individualized experience with a unique foundation. Finally, keeping a spiritual journal allows you to keep track of your progress.

Meet People

You should still make an effort to get to know other eclectic Wiccans or those who share a similar set of beliefs. You can join Facebook groups or other social media communities or get together with informal Pagan groups in your area. This way, you can chat with others and get to know them without joining a coven. If you don't have any local groups, you can create your own safe space or get-togethers for like-minded individuals.

Don't Be Afraid to Ask Questions

Everyone starts somewhere. If you really want to learn and expand your knowledge, you must ask the right questions. Pay attention to what aspects interest you and ask around about the topics you wish to learn more about. In addition, be open to other perspectives and differing opinions. If someone says something that contradicts the information you already have, discuss it with them and conduct your own research. Don't take every piece of information as it is, and always remember that your experience is probably a lot different than those around you. This means that not everything you read or hear will resonate with you. Ask others for valid and accurate resources and dig deep into things you're skeptical about.

Keep Learning

You can never know too much in the world of spirituality and religion. Always be keen on learning and asking others for recommendations regarding resources and books that you can learn from. If you read something you enjoy, you can search for similar books, articles, or other pieces written by the same author. You should also aim to learn through your own experience and interactions with others.

Eclectic Solitary Practice

Luckily for you, practicing as a solitary Wiccan works best for eclectic traditions and practices. Many people who practice spirituality and religion on their own find that structured belief systems don't work well for them. They benefit more from developing new beliefs and traditions on their own. Being an eclectic Wiccan in solitary allows you to blend your own convictions with pre-established traditions to create a system that suits your needs. This way, you don't have to adopt a tradition just because it works for another individual or a group of people. You can replace the initiation ritual with a self-dedication one if you wish. This ritual can mark your commitment to your deities, beliefs, spiritual growth, and of course, the entire journey.

Eclectic Covens

If solitary practice isn't the path for you, you should consider joining a coven. Unfortunately, many Wiccans and Pagans don't publicly advertise their beliefs, so you may find it hard to come across groves, temples, and other places of worship. This is why networking is key when it comes to NeoPagan group practices. You need to put in a lot of effort to let like-minded people know that you wish to join a group. After spreading the word, a local group might reach out to you. Networking websites can also help, as long as you take the necessary precautions when meeting people you got to know online.

Keep in mind that some covens may be gender-specific, while others can be family-oriented or made particularly for members of the LGBTQ+ community. Some covens may also have a set limit for the number of members who can join. So, you need to make sure that the covens you find are suitable for you and have members you can get along with in terms of philosophies and personalities. Remember, coven members are a lot like family members. It might take you some time to feel accepted and comfortable.

In this chapter, we have discussed:

- Eclectic Wicca is a very comprehensive and all-embracing term.

- It is typically used to reference witchcraft activities and Wiccan traditions, especially those of the NeoWiccans that don't fall into a particular category of practice.

- Most Wiccans who live in non-pagan communities usually walk the eclectic path. However, many covens also consider themselves eclectic practitioners of Wicca.

- There are several things you can do to ensure that your journey as a solitary eclectic Wiccan is successful. This includes setting up a daily routine, keeping a spiritual diary, meeting other NeoWiccans, and being an avid learner.

- While it can be hard to find one that suits you, you can join an eclectic coven if practicing in solitary isn't right for you.

The next chapter covers what covens are and how you can choose the right members in more depth. Reading it, you will also discover the pros and cons of practicing in solitary.

Chapter 3: The Overview of Wiccan Covens, Circles, and Solitary Practitioners

"The practice of magic is not evil or destructive—Witches and folk magicians, through timeless rituals, are only drawing upon natural energies found within the earth and our bodies to create positive, life-affirming change." — Scott Cunningham

A Deeper Look into the Wicca Practice

Prepare to unleash the witch in you! This is probably one of the most interesting chapters since we discuss different methods to practice witchcraft. We cover everything you need to know about covens. We also talk you through the Wiccan circle and how to cast one. Since coven life isn't for everyone, we offer insight into other alternatives like solitary practice and what you need to know if you choose to be a solitary practitioner.

An Introduction to Covens

A coven is a small group of witches who get together to practice witchcraft. The members don't have to be a specific number, but some covens usually form groups of 13. The witches in a coven often become very close and consider each other best friends or even family. For this reason, many people refer to Wicca as a family religion. Before choosing a coven or initiating members to one, spend some time with them to make sure everyone gets along and is compatible with each other.

The meeting place of a coven is called covenstead, and a covendom is an area served by a covenstead. All coven members should live within a close radius of their covendom. Additionally, it is essential that covendoms do not overlap, so covens should always be six miles apart. However, nowadays, modern covens don't follow this rule.

The Coven Life

Witches get together in a coven to work on their witchcraft skills, practice spells, rituals, and help each other with complicated spells. Although you should be compatible with your coven members, you don't need to have similar practices. In fact, this can be beneficial to you, especially as a beginner. You will learn from different types of witches and grow stronger as a coven.

Coven meetings usually start and end with a ritual. The ritual performed depends on the phase of the moon and the time of year. A coven would usually meet and perform a ritual when a problem arises. Members of a Wiccan coven usually meet for Sabbats to celebrate seasonal festivals.

We mentioned that covens value their privacy, so members cannot give information about their meetings or whereabouts to anyone outside the coven. If you must tell someone for whatever reason, you must consult with your High Priest or High Priestess first.

Traditional Coven Structures

Much like in a company, there is a hierarchy and structure within the coven. There should be two leaders: a High Priest and a High Priestess representing God and Goddess. As mentioned in chapter one, sometimes these leaders are elected for one year, as the Seax Wicca tradition allows, and they can also be re-elected. For covens that don't hold elections, the choice for the next leader falls on the sitting High Priest/Priestess before they resign. Additionally, leaders should be called High Priests and High Priestesses even when they are no longer in position.

As explained earlier in the book, initiates can be promoted in some traditions like the Alexandrian and Gardnerian traditions. For instance, in Gardnerian Wicca, "first degree" usually refers to ritual chorus participants. According to the Gardnerian rules, a member must spend at least a year and a day in the chorus before advancing to the second and third degrees. As you progress, you start participating in more rituals. When a witch reaches the third degree, they have the option to break away from the coven.

However, all covens are different. Some have more or less than three degrees, or demand initiates spend a long time between degrees. It is important to note that covens are led, not ruled - this isn't royalty - and there isn't one person who leads all witches.

Each tradition has a set of rules that govern its coven to ensure harmony between its members. For instance, in the Gardnerian tradition, the High Priest and High Priestess are the ones that govern the coven. They can also be stripped of their ranks if necessary to ensure peace. Just like leaders are punished, members of the coven can be banished, but it requires unanimous voting.

Newer Adaptations

Everything moves with the times, and Wicca covens are no different. Now practitioners take advantage of technology and the internet by establishing online covens. Witches also meet on social media platforms like Facebook groups, where they can agree to get together to go hiking or howl at the moon. The internet will give you the chance to find other witches and covens in your area. That said, the internet isn't always a safe option, so caution is advised.

The Wiccan Circle

When performing a spell or a ritual, you should form a circle with your other coven members. However, some require circles depending on the tradition you follow, while others don't. According to witchcraft oral history, circles are used to define a sacred area. Additionally, they also keep unwanted energy away while you are practicing magic. Even if you are a solitary practitioner, you should still create a circle when it is required.

Before forming a circle, you will first need to know its purpose and how many people will be in it - this will help you determine its size. For instance, small coven meetings won't require more than a nine-foot diameter circle. You will also need to choose the spot where you will cast your circle. Depending on your tradition, you can draw it on the ground, or you and your coven can simply visualize it. Your circle should be positioned according to the four cardinal points. You can place a marker like a candle at the north, south, east, and west.

Casting the circle will also depend on your tradition. For instance, some traditions require you to call upon the God and Goddess to join the rituals, whereas, in other traditions, the High Priest or High Priestess are the ones who call upon the gods. They will do the calling in each of the four directions, starting at the north. The ritual should then commence.

None of the members should leave the circle once it is closed. However, if you must leave, you will need to practice something called "ceremonial cutting." TAn athame is used to make a cutting motion in the circle to your right, then to your left. You will have to re-enter the circle the same way and reconnect its lines. After you finish your spell or ritual, clear the circle the same way you cast it, but this time the High Priest/Priestess will politely dismiss the gods and thank them for guarding the coven.

Solitary Practice

Not everyone is comfortable with practicing magic in groups or covens, or they may not have the option to join one. In these cases, they begin solitary practice. Solitary practice is simply practicing spells, rituals, or spiritual faith alone at home or any place of your choice. You don't need to be a part of a coven or join other witches to practice magic, and you can still participate in certain activities like the Sabbats. Whether you choose solitary practice or to be part of a coven, there is no right or wrong here. They each have their advantages and disadvantages so just go with whatever feels right. If you change your mind, you can always join a coven and vice versa.

You can practice any of the popular traditions mentioned in the first chapter. However, many solitary practitioners prefer to follow the path of eclectic Wicca (discussed in depth in the previous chapter). Choose whatever works for you.

Reasons for Choosing a Solitary Path

There are various reasons to choose a solitary path, like working in the privacy of your home, at your own pace, and around your own schedule. If you are an introvert, this path will be perfect for you since you won't have to interact with people you don't know. That said, it doesn't matter whether you are an introvert or extrovert. Some witches like to work alone to establish their own witchcraft without outside influence. Additionally, solitary practice will give you the chance to learn about yourself, which will make you a more powerful witch in the long run.

One thing that makes many people choose this path is the freedom to make up their own rules. For instance, you can change your practice whenever you want, you can also perform any kind of magic like cursing or hexing, or if you don't want to perform these spells, you don't need to cave under pressure and do something against your morals. Unleash your rebellious spirit and march to the beat of your own drum.

Bear in mind solitary practice has its disadvantages as well. Working with other witches will help you gain more knowledge and experience, which will aid in your growth as a witch. So, carefully consider both options before making a decision.

Tips for Solitary Practitioners

If you want to be a solitary practitioner, you should keep a few things in mind.

- Make practice and studying part of your daily routine. When you are alone, you may lack the motivation or encouragement a group can provide to practice rituals, spells, or meditate. Therefore, create a schedule with tasks to do every day to help you progress.

- Keep a journal or your own Book of Shadows. You must keep a record of your magical studies. There will always be spells and rituals that work and others that don't, and this journal will help you in the future as a reference. Additionally, documenting everything will help you lay down the basics for your tradition, and you can refer back to it at any time.

- Keep reading, studying, and learning. Ask your Wiccan friends for book recommendations. When you read a book you like, check to see other books by the same author. Reading is the best way to expand your knowledge.

- Understand that it is ok to ask questions and be skeptical of anything you read. If something doesn't sit right with you or you aren't convinced, ask other practitioners for their take or conduct more research on the topic. It doesn't matter if it is written in a book; it still won't make it valid. Questioning everything is how you learn and grow.

- Try to meet other Wiccans and Pagans. Choosing solitary practice doesn't mean that you should avoid socializing with people of a similar background. Even if you don't have any Wiccan friends, you can check Facebook or any other online resources, as mentioned earlier, to find others in your area. This isn't similar to joining a coven; you simply interact with people who share your interests. Talking to them allows you to discuss things that no one else can understand, and you have someone to turn to when seeking help with aspects you are struggling with.

In this chapter, we have discussed:

- Covens, what they are, and how to choose the right members

- The structure of a traditional coven and how High Priests and High Priestesses are considered the highest degree. Also covered is how they are chosen and how you can advance in a coven

- Online covens and using the internet to find other Wiccans

- The Wiccan circle, why you need it, and how you can cast one

- Solitary practice, what it is, its advantages, why this may be the path for you, and tips for solitary practitioners of all traditions

If you are going to be a Wiccan witch and practice magic, you need to know everything about covens and solitary practice to decide which path is right for you. Remember, this is all down to personal preference, and as we have mentioned, you can always go back. You also need to learn how to cast a Wiccan circle as it is vital to both a coven and solitary practitioner.

Whatever path you choose, each one has its advantages and disadvantages. In this chapter, we emphasized the pros and cons of being a solo practitioner while introducing you to the life and structure of a coven. In the next chapter, we go over the benefits and drawbacks of joining a coven in detail so you can make an informed decision.

Chapter 4: The Pros and Cons of Covens

"You needed at least three witches for a coven. Two witches was just an argument."

— Terry Pratchett

The concept of covens, also commonly known as gatherings and circles, goes back to a woman named Margaret Murray. In the 1920s, Murray decided that all witches must meet up in groups containing 13 individuals each. This idea was based on the belief that each member (there are supposedly 12 witches and 1 Devil) had to specialize in a certain magical practice. This meant that each group, as a whole, possessed a wide array of talents, signaling their power or greatness. So instead of networking to build connections, witches interacted for power.

Fortunately, the idea behind covens has evolved significantly throughout the years. Covens are now not just a teaching or learning place, but they have also become an opportunity to connect with like-minded individuals and build supportive communities. It has since developed to reference a group of at least 3 witches who came together for a single purpose or goal. Smaller covens are typically more organized and controlled. Larger ones, however, are high energy and give a greater sense of support. The goal behind each coven depends on the convictions of its founders.

If you do not wish to practice eclectic Wicca in solitary, you can join an existing coven or create your own group. Covens come in various structures, depending on their primary purpose. For instance, new members learn from older and more experienced ones in Teach Covens, while Community-Only Circles don't aim to teach but are created to contribute to the sense of community. Examples of other covens include Deity Covens, Men's Only Covens, Women's Only Covens, Online Covens, and more. Basically, there is a coven for everyone.

Each gathering has a unique hierarchy. For instance, some covens may follow a High Priest or High Priestess, and others may give older members seniority over the younger and newer ones. The purpose behind the latter structure is to pass on the teachings, traditions, and culture of the coven and ensure its longevity and continuity. Most of the covens that follow this system require new members to perform traditional rites before becoming permanent participants. These rites can be anything, depending on the decision of the coven's founder and its existing members. For example, some covens request that temporary members complete a specified learning level, complete a traditional year, or attend a certain number of meetings before they can attend rituals. Other circles don't have a set hierarchy. Instead, they allow the group members to build natural connections and relationships. These groups usually don't have restrictions or requirements regarding who can join.

However, any coven (at least the ones that are worth joining) come with a set of rules and regulations. These rules are generally fair and created to ensure the group remains a safe and appropriate space for all its members. We advise against joining covens that don't come with a good set of rules as they often don't last and end up running into trouble. In this chapter, we'll explore the pros and cons of joining a coven, as well as a few things to keep in mind before you make a decision.

Reasons to Join a Coven

We've touched on the benefits of practicing in solitary and covered some of the ways you can make sure that your journey is as fruitful as possible in chapter 2. Now, it's time to explore some of the reasons why you should consider joining a coven. This will help you decide whether you wish to embark on your spiritual path solo or with a support group by your side.

Enriching Learning Opportunities

One of the main reasons you should consider joining a coven is that it offers an enriched learning opportunity. Books, the web, and documentaries can be valuable sources of information. However, there are some things that you just won't know or understand unless someone guides and shows you. People who practice in solitary, especially if they've been doing it for years, often believe they know plenty. Joining a coven typically proves them wrong. Circles allow you to learn from experienced eclectic Wiccans, as they have accumulated a great deal of wisdom and knowledge over the years. Covens expand your views and allow you to challenge your ideologies and limitations.

Networking and Connections

If none of your friends and family understand Wicca, you will eventually feel the strong need to connect with people who do. You will feel a strong sense of relief, happiness, and excitement once you meet someone who shares the same views as you. You'll get to go to festivals and partake in events and rituals that you otherwise wouldn't have known about. As we mentioned earlier in the book, you can get involved with the community as a solitary. However, it's much easier and more fun when you already know some of the people who will be attending.

A Source of Support

Not everyone understands Wicca and Paganism. To begin with, some traditional Wiccans aren't even convinced with eclectic and NeoWicca. This means that the further you walk into your spiritual journey, the more your beliefs, traditions, and convictions will be challenged. Covens offer a great deal of mental, physical, emotional, and spiritual support throughout your growth, development, and experimentation period. They provide strength and security whenever you need it the most, allowing you to push through and stay resilient.

Accountability and Consistency

As you may recall, one of the hardest things about being a solitary practitioner is holding yourself accountable and staying consistent with your spiritual progress. It's so easy to skip the festivals and other events when you're practicing alone. However, covens typically set up calendars and schedules for meet-ups, festivals, and other important events. Some circles even provide homework assignment readings to ensure everyone is up to speed. Covens often designate tasks to their members throughout the year. Each coven comes with its own expectations regarding the participation and attendance of all members. The longer you stay in the circle, the more responsibilities and expectations fall on you.

Cons of Joining a Coven

Just like joining a coven has its pros, it also has its cons. It's important to be informed on the cons to help you decide what is best for you. The disadvantages of becoming a member include:

Traditional Hierarchy

As we explained above, many covens are structured in hierarchical systems. If you don't work well in spaces with senior figures or any kind of authority, then you may struggle to find a coven that suits your needs. If you tend to be the leader of your groups, then you may find this hierarchical structure a little confining and discouraging. While it may benefit you to learn from others, you may feel frustrated when it's time to abide by the rules or if your insights aren't taken seriously.

Disagreements

Not everyone has the same exact set of convictions and philosophies. This is especially the case when it comes to eclectic Wicca. As you know, this belief system allows its practitioners flexibility in terms of traditions, insights, and modifications. Unfortunately, you usually have to participate in pre-existing rituals, festivals, events, and traditions with covens. This leaves very few opportunities for individuality, which defies the purpose of eclecticism. If you don't trust the source of information or are skeptical regarding the validity of their teachings, you will also find it hard to cope.

Expectations, Responsibilities, and Regulations

While these were all mentioned as pros, they can also be the downside of joining a coven. Responsibilities and expectations, such as obligatory attendances and task allocation, can be very binding. It makes sense that you need to show up if you wish to be part of the group. However, if you struggle with your mental health or have other duties like work and family to take care of, you can find it hard to stay on top of your coven schedule.

Inner Cliques

Every group has its own inner groups. As a new member, expect to find cliques and don't expect everyone to like you. You may feel ostracized and therefore discouraged to participate in spiritual activities with the group.

Other Things to Keep in Mind

As explained before, a coven is a witch's or a Wiccan's family. Many circles function on that basis. This makes it very hard to find your place as a new member in a coven. In retrospect, not all coven members act like family, making it hard to build very strong ties and bonds with them. You will undoubtedly meet coven mates who will grow to become a very important part of your life. You will be able to build a sense of trust, love, and respect toward them and receive these things in return. However, it may take you a lot of time and effort to find these people. This is why it's very important to think about what you expect from a coven and its members. Do you want to join a circle that operates as a family, or do you wish to build relationships with people of your own accord? Having clear expectations and setting up strong boundaries is crucial when you join a coven.

Another thing you must keep in mind is that some covens are temporary. They are built to fulfill a particular purpose, and once it's achieved, the coven is dissolved. This is something to consider upon choosing a coven to join. You don't want to become a member thinking that this circle will last for years and years to come, just to find out that you're the only person who thinks that way.

When joining a coven, you will likely be asked plenty of questions by the leader or its members. These questions will probably revolve around your ideologies, spirituality, your expectations regarding the circle, why you chose to join it, and how you found out about it. Asking your own questions is also a good idea. Here are a few questions you should consider asking:

- Which traditions and beliefs does this eclectic Wiccan coven mainly incorporate? What principle tenets does it have?

- What is expected of the coven members?

- How often do the members meet, and how great are the responsibilities they need to take on?

- Do I need to make financial contributions?

- Is attendance mandatory?

- Are there any rules and regulations that I need to be aware of?

- If this coven kept a secret? If so, why is it?

- What are the reasons you would exclude anyone from this coven?

- How can I join and leave this coven?

In this chapter, we have discussed:

- Just like you can benefit greatly from practicing eclectic Wicca in solitary, you can find joining a coven a very fulfilling and worthwhile experience.

- There are numerous advantages to joining a circle, including the abundance of learning opportunities and resources, building strong connections, having a support system, and maintaining consistency.

- Like any other group membership, however, joining a coven has its drawbacks and rules you just can't get behind. These include rigid hierarchical systems, possible disagreements, meeting certain expectations, and the need to take on responsibilities.

- If you decide to join a coven, make sure you narrow down your choices by asking the aforementioned questions.

In the next chapter, you'll discover the steps to finding your spiritual path.

Chapter 5: How to Find Your Wiccan Path?

"The spiritual journey is individual, highly personal. It can't be organized or regulated. It isn't true that everyone should follow one path. Listen to your own truth."

— Ram Dass

Many organized religions and belief systems are concerned with converting you first and letting you verse yourself into the details later. Wicca, on the other hand, is an experiential religion. As flexible and relieving as that sounds, individuals who are used to being told what to do often feel challenged. Many people rush to purchase all the tools they can find, learn all the spells they come across, and hold rituals. While these are all things that you will get to do sooner or later, you need to start at a much slower pace. This chapter breaks down the process of finding one's Wiccan path into a simple step-by-step rundown.

Read, Read, and Read

If you're reading this book, then you've already gotten a head start on this step. You need to read extensively about the various aspects of Wicca before you seriously consider converting. Finding your Wiccan path is a decision and process that needs contemplation. It's not something that you can take lightly. Chances are you won't be able to get very far in Wicca if you're not fond of reading and researching.

This is because, as we mentioned above, this religion doesn't tell you what to do. Instead, it allows you to explore and decide for yourself, which requires much knowledge. You can't just read one book and decide that you're ready to dive right in. Start by reading five or ten books, then go from there. Many experienced Wiccans suggest spending at least a year studying and reading about Wicca. Afterward, take a day to finally decide whether Wicca is the right choice for you. Read books and articles that give you insight into what it's like to be Wiccan, how your life will change, and the kind of lifestyle you will lead. Read about other people's experiences and how this decision affected various aspects of their lives, negatively and positively.

Contemplate

As you start reading about Wicca and its aspects, you need to consider whether these beliefs and tenets match your principles and worldview. While eclectic Wicca allows you to personalize the experience, you still need to resonate with the core framework of Wicca. Although this religion doesn't come with commandments and scriptures, it still isn't anything you want it to be. If it's anything and everything, then it's nothing. For instance, some people, who don't believe in deities and don't plan to worship them, decide to become Wiccan because they're interested in magic. If they don't resonate with the essence of Wicca, then why should they partake in festivals, rituals, and rites when they can study Witchcraft alone? The great thing about Wicca is that it isn't a take it or leave it sort of philosophy. However, it makes sense to use reason and logic, especially since it's an experiential religion. Don't force it to work if it doesn't. You can find other belief systems that are aligned with your ideals.

Start Praying

After you think about your idea of Wicca and determine which deities you wish to worship, it's time to start praying for them. Introduce yourself to them and kindly ask them to come forward and reveal themselves to you. Ask them to clarify things for you, help you understand things that you can't quite grasp, and guide you on your spiritual journey. Incorporate meditation into your daily practice. People say that you talk to your deity when you pray, but you listen to them when you meditate. Not only will daily meditation help you improve your spirituality, but it will also help boost your overall wellness and health.

Come Up with a Self-Dedication Ritual

Now that you feel certain about embarking on your Wiccan journey and connected with your deity, you need to come up with a ritual that allows you to dedicate yourself to the Wiccan way of life. There is no right or wrong way to do this. You need to find your own spiritual balance with the world around you. Here, you need to remember the principles of this religion, which include respecting and honoring the divine and doing whatever feels right to you as long as you don't harm any living thing. Your ritual has to be true to you and fulfill your needs. You can create a ritual from scratch or take bits and pieces from the things you read. You can even follow another individual's self-dedication ritual. It's all acceptable as long as it resonates with you and reflects your wish to dedicate yourself to the religion.

Take the Time to Observe

You need to observe life from the perspective of a Wiccan. This means that you should start paying special attention to the cycles of seasons and those of the moon. Acknowledge these changes and the cyclical nature of life. Whenever you come face to face with an obstacle or have a decision to make, think about how you would approach them through Wiccan ethics and tenets. Contemplate the many areas of your life where you can learn and apply the lessons that Wicca has to teach. Observe life and the environment around you. Watch how all living things interact to sustain life. Observe and partake in life and its cycles. Don't stop learning and reading, but begin applying the knowledge you have gained to your life. Celebrate the Sabbats and Esbats by conducting informal life or consistently praying and meditating. Embrace life as a Wiccan.

Be Mindful

When getting started in Wicca, many people make the mistake of rushing to buy every tool that they can think of. Collecting tools is a very exciting and important part of the Wicca practice. Upon reading into Wicca, you will also find multiple books urging you to go out and buy all the tools it mentions. However, you need to remind yourself that you don't need to purchase everything all at once. It helps to look into each tool and understand its purpose. Think about what you need it for, whether you need it now, and how frequently you will be incorporating it into your practice. You can look for it, or even build it yourself, then start to use it. Take the time to explore each tool on its own. Take it one step at a time. You will come to realize that many of the tools you come across won't serve your needs.

At this point, you need to begin cultivating a more mindful approach toward your practice and rituals. You don't need to plan everything down to the last detail. However, by definition, keep in mind that rituals are repetitive practices. You become more conscious of your rituals through repetition. If you are mindful and actively thinking about conducting your rituals correctly, you will finally be able to go beyond that state of consciousness. After repeating them enough times, you can go into "autopilot" mode. Only then will you be able to open yourself up to the higher vibrations by getting out of your head and into your body. Take the time to think about invocations, casting circles, and opening and closing rituals. You don't need to do this every day. However, once you feel like you've gotten the hang of your current practices, add another element to the process.

Practice Magic

While magic is a huge part of Wicca, it isn't necessarily its center of attention. Sooner or later, you will have to incorporate some elements of magic into your spiritual practice. As we mentioned above, magic and witchcraft aren't exclusive to Wicca. If you're only interested in becoming a witch, you don't have to become Wiccan. You can skip straight to the craft itself. However, if you're taking up Wicca for its beliefs and tenets, and not just because you're interested in magic, you first have to familiarize yourself with the religion. You can't practice magic right away. Once you have a good set of tools to work with and have already relatively mastered the art of holding rituals on a regular basis, then you're ready to start exploring this mystical element. Start studying the art of magic and begin reading about it. You don't want to mess things up, which is why you need to go slow and implement only small workings of magic into your circle.

Will You Join a Coven or Practice in Solitary?

After exploring everything this religion has to offer, you need to decide how to practice. This is something that the previous chapters can also help with. Go over the pros and cons of joining a coven and compare them with those of practicing in solitary so you can come to a decision. Remember that if one method doesn't work for you, you can always try another. As we explained in chapter 2, there are numerous types of covens out there. This is why you need to select one that aligns with your personality and philosophy. If you'd like to practice in solitary, you must always find ways to enrich your knowledge. You can sign up for online newsletters, browse articles on the internet, participate in forums, and read books and magazines regarding Wicca and its community.

Get to Know the Community

We've already stressed the importance of networking and connecting with other Wiccans multiple times in the book. However, it's worth mentioning again since it is important to find your Wiccan path. You will learn many things through interacting with others that you would have never known on your own.

In this chapter, we have discussed:

- If you're considering becoming Wiccan, you're probably struggling to pinpoint where to start.

- The great thing about Wicca is that there aren't rules or instructions you need to follow when it comes to the things you should do.

- No one will tell you that you're worshipping the "wrong" deity and that you should honor another instead. You won't be handed a rigid set of rules or guidelines regarding what you're expected to do either. You won't be turned away if your beliefs and convictions differ from others'.

- Generally speaking, reading, contemplating, praying, observing, practicing mindfulness, and exploring magic will help guide you on your journey.

"Wicca is an inward journey as much as it is outward." —
Anujj Elviis

We can use many words to describe Wicca, like Deities, magic, and rituals. However, we can't think of a better way to sum it up than this: Wicca is the family religion that brings people closer together. One of the things that caught our attention while writing this book, and has probably caught yours as well now that you have finished it, is that Wicca brings people from different backgrounds, genders, and sexual orientations together. It turns strangers to family, which is the coven life for you.

Learning about its origins and how it came to be is the best way to understand anything, whether it be a tradition, movement, or religion. This is why we have dedicated the first chapter to the many traditions of Wicca. Understanding how each one started and what they are all about will help you discover the history of your new belief system so you can choose the right path for you. Wicca is a rich religion with its different Deities, practices, and traditions, and familiarizing yourself with this information is the first step on your journey.

We have also included Eclectic Wicca, which is a more modern and less traditional path. Whether you will be a coven or solitary practitioner, you can choose any of the traditions we have provided in this book. We have given you all the information you will need to grow as a witch confidently. Whatever you choose, make sure the path speaks to you and feels right - This is about feeling comfortable and safe where you find your calling.

You can practice witchcraft in solitary or in a coven. Each has its advantages and disadvantages. This mainly depends on you, your personality, and what you are comfortable with. We have researched everything you need to know about coven life, the coven hierarchy, and how to choose your coven members. We also debate the benefits and drawbacks of joining a coven while offering some words of caution.

All the information you need to know about solitary practice is laid out in this book, including its pros and cons, as well as tips to help you out if you decide to take this path. We ended the book with a chapter dedicated to finding your Wiccan path. To better understand Wicca, you must keep reading and never stop learning or practicing. This will illuminate your way to affirm your path or perhaps choose a new one. We have discussed your ancestors and tips to help you find the right coven and resources to help get you started as a solitary witch.

In this book, we have worked very hard to help get you started as a Wicca beginner and put you on the right track. However, reading this book is merely the first step. You need to get out there and practice everything you have read. Find a coven so you can grow as a witch or study and learn to become a solo practitioner to better learn about yourself. You need to speak with other Wiccans and learn from their journey and experience. Remember, never stop questioning and seeking answers and new perspectives. We weren't put on this planet to accept everything at face value. We are witches, born with a rebellious spirit and a desire to open our minds and hearts to everything around us.

References

Berger, H. A., Resident Scholar, & Brandeis University. (2022, February 16). Here's why your pre-sleep routine matters.

Harrow, J. (2002). Wicca covens: How to start and organize your own. Citadel Press.

Why teens are attracted to Wicca. (2019, August 31). Focus on the Family. https://www.focusonthefamily.com/parenting/why-teens-are-attracted-to-wicca/

Wicca Quotes. (n.d.). Goodreads.Com. Retrieved from https://www.goodreads.com/quotes/tag/wicca

Wigington, P. (n.d.-a). 5 tips for practicing as a solitary wiccan or pagan. Learn Religions. Retrieved from https://www.learnreligions.com/practicing-as-a-solitary-pagan-2562542

Wigington, P. (n.d.-b). Eclectic Wicca. Learn Religions. Retrieved from https://www.learnreligions.com/eclectic-wicca-2562909

witchcraft - Contemporary witchcraft. (n.d.). In Encyclopedia Britannica.

Introduction to Faery & Celtic Witchcraft. (2020, June 18). ToSalem. https://tosalem.com/introduction-to-faery-celtic-witchcraft/

Norse Paganism for beginners: Quick recap + resources. (2021, June 20). Time Nomads | Your Pagan Store Online. https://www.timenomads.com/norse-paganism-for-beginners/

Reading the runes: The viking runic alphabet - 'futhark,' history and meanings. (n.d.). Happy Piranha. Retrieved from https://happypiranha.com/blogs/news/reading-the-runes-the-viking-runic-alphabet-futhark-history-and-meanings

Top 6 quotes of GERALD GARDNER famous quotes and sayings. (n.d.). Inspiring Quotes. Retrieved from https://www.inspiringquotes.us/author/8431-gerald-gardner

Wicca, Gardnerian Wicca, Wiccan, Witchcraft, Bude, boscastle - North Cornwall Gardnerian Wicca/coven, Bude. (n.d.). Hugofox.Com. Retrieved from https://www.hugofox.com/community/north-cornwall-gardnerian-wicca-coven-14824/what-is-wicca

Wiccan traditions - seax-Wicca - SunSigns.Org. (2015, February 12). Sun Signs. https://www.sunsigns.org/wiccan-traditions-seax-wicca/

Wigington, P. (n.d.-a). Alexandrian Wicca. Learn Religions. Retrieved from https://www.learnreligions.com/alexandrian-wicca-2562902

Wigington, P. (n.d.-b). Dianic Wicca. Learn Religions. Retrieved from https://www.learnreligions.com/what-is-dianic-wicca-2562908

Wigington, P. (n.d.-c). Gerald Gardner and the gardnerian Wiccan tradition. Learn Religions. Retrieved from https://www.learnreligions.com/what-is-gardnerian-wicca-2562910

WiseWitch. (2018, February 7). Seax Wicca (Saxon Wicca). Wise Witches and Witchcraft. https://witchcraftandwitches.com/types-of-wicca/seax-saxon-wicca/

Wigington, P. (n.d.-a). 5 tips for practicing as a solitary wiccan or pagan. Retrieved from Learn Religions website: https://www.learnreligions.com/practicing-as-a-solitary-pagan-2562542

Wigington, P. (n.d.-b). Eclectic Wicca. Retrieved from Learn Religions website: https://www.learnreligions.com/eclectic-wicca-2562909

Wigington, P. (n.d.-c). How to find a coven near you. Retrieved from Learn Religions website: https://www.learnreligions.com/how-to-find-a-coven-2562078

Eckardt, S. (2018, October 30). How to become a witch: A beginner's guide. W Magazine. https://www.wmagazine.com/story/how-to-become-a-witch-beginners-guide

Kyteler, E. (2020, May 20). Solitary witch: 5 reasons you should practice alone. Eclectic Witchcraft. https://eclecticwitchcraft.com/solitary-witch-practice-alone/

May, A. (2019, November 20). What's a Wiccan coven? 7 fantastic little-known facts. Welcome To Wicca Now. https://wiccanow.com/whats-a-wiccan-coven-7-fantastic-little-known-facts/

What is the difference between covendom and coven? (2014, June 19). WikiDiff. https://wikidiff.com/covendom/coven

What's trending today. (n.d.). My Trending Stories. Retrieved from https://mytrendingstories.com/kalaeo-nox/everything-you-need-to-know-about-covens

Wicca Quotes. (n.d.). Goodreads.Com. Retrieved from https://www.goodreads.com/quotes/tag/wicca

Wigington, P. (n.d.-a). 5 tips for practicing as a solitary wiccan or pagan. Learn Religions. Retrieved from https://www.learnreligions.com/practicing-as-a-solitary-pagan-2562542

Wigington, P. (n.d.-b). How to cast a circle as a sacred space. Learn Religions. Retrieved from https://www.learnreligions.com/how-to-cast-a-circle-2562859

Cultivatemagick. (2020, September 16). Which is better: Coven or Solitary Witchcraft? Retrieved from The Spiritual Garden website: https://www.cultivatemagick.com/covens-versus-solitary-witches/

The Witches Next Door. (2017, November 8). Should I join A coven? A few things to consider. Retrieved from The Witches Next Door website: https://www.patheos.com/blogs/thewitchesnextdoor/2017/11/joining-a-coven/

Wyrd, A. (2020, March 26). 5 reasons you should join a coven. Retrieved from Exemplore website: https://exemplore.com/wicca-witchcraft/5-Reasons-Why-You-Should-Join-a-Coven

Pollux, A. (2019, October 16). Wicca for beginners – 9 Amazing Tips for becoming Wiccan. Retrieved from Welcome To Wicca Now website: https://wiccanow.com/wicca-for-beginners-becoming-wiccan/

Wright, M. S. (2013, August 5). Becoming wiccan: 7 useful steps to start you on your path. Retrieved from Exemplore website: https://exemplore.com/wicca-witchcraft/How-to-Become-Wiccan-Taking-the-First-Steps-on-your-Path

Book 2: Candle Magic for Beginners

"Look at how a single candle can both defy and define the darkness." – Anne Frank.

Anne Frank's words carry more truth to them than most people could imagine. We use candles to cast light when it's dark to see and find our way. Yet, despite this happening on the physical plane, candles can also be used to illuminate our spiritual plane. We all have darkness within us and surrounding us, but not in the physical sense. Anger, frustration, sadness, hate, jealousy, anxiety, and fear, that's the darkness within. The negative energy of some people you come in contact with and the horrible things that happen everywhere around us in the world that's the darkness surrounding us on emotional and spiritual levels. Candles can help you cast light and navigate your way through both.

For most people, candles are mere tools that we rarely use in our everyday lives. For witches, they are an integral part of their daily routine. The practice of using candle magick to bring about change in your life has been around for centuries. Many civilizations understood the power that a single candle holds and the changes it can manifest on the physical plane. Whether it's your fear of the future or years of suffering from low self-esteem, a candle can help you overcome that spiritual and emotional turmoil. It can help you shield yourself from that coworker's negative energy and the jealous relative's ill intentions toward you. A candle can help you heal from past traumas and grow emotionally, can help you find love, attract money and wealth, or even a job.

Candles can change your life, provided you have enough belief and understanding.

In this book, you will learn about the ancient practice of using candles to heal your pain — physically, emotionally, and spiritually. You will learn to perform rituals and cast spells that can attract the things you want in life and banish those that no longer serve you. Every human out there has a list of wishes and dreams, as well as fears and pain. What few understand, however, is that you can control those things. You are in charge of your fate. You can banish the things holding you back and attract love, abundance, and happiness. With this book as your resource, you'll understand how you can do every one of those things.

I have spent many years researching and understanding these ancient witchcraft practices and its more modern movements, namely, Wicca. Contrary to popular beliefs, as a religion, Wicca aims to help people become happier versions of themselves. Witches promote a healthy lifestyle and a positive outlook on life. With the help of spells and rituals like the ones I will outline in this book, witches have managed to leverage the power of candles to bring about positive change into their lives. The spells I have curated in this book are carefully selected and curated to help anyone turn their life around. You don't have to be an experienced witch to perform the candle magick outlined here. If this is your first brush with these practices, you can still successfully get what you want if you follow my instructions.

I chose to write a book on this matter to help as many people harvest and utilize this ancient knowledge to simply become happier. I sought to put down my extensive expertise and insights into the world of spiritualism and Wicca in a simple, easy-to-use guide on candle magick, one of the most powerful tools at a witch's disposal, which can be read and practiced by anyone.

All you need is to keep an open mind and to be willing to try, and you'll learn everything you need to know about candle magick, starting with its origins and how each candle color means something, which you'll learn in the first chapter.

Chapter 1: Understanding Candle Magic

"The most tangible of all visible mysteries — fire." – Leigh Hunt.

Candle magic is a form of fire magic, and the importance of fire dates back to the earliest records we have of humans. As early as ancient man, humans have found a source of comfort and inspiration in the flames of a fire. It inspired awe and a sense of wonder in early men with its ability to keep them warm and cook food while also providing protection. To this very day, fire performs the same functions. Candles weren't around back then, but fires were used in ceremonial rituals like Samhain, where large bonfires were used to celebrate the occasion and commemorate the day.

The power of a flame to illuminate the darkness meant that when candles were invented, they had religious significance for many ancient civilizations. One of the oldest civilizations known to man, Ancient Egypt, had several gods and goddesses to whom homage was paid using candles. Followers of the goddess Isis placed candles all around her temples to be lit every hour of every day to symbolize constant light and hope. For pagans, it was Sabbat, which involved using candles with the Yule tree. For Wiccans, several ceremonies require the use of candles as a symbol of fire, one of the main elements from which witches draw power and energy. Even Christianity used candles on altars as part of the religion's rituals.

Candle Magic

Despite candle magick being associated with the fire element, it's actually more than that. Candle magick is alchemy for many witches – a combination of several elements. The candle flame is fire, the oxygen that feeds the flame is air, the wax that melts symbolizes water, and the wax that congeals is earth. Imbued with powerful and clear intentions, candle magick can then leverage the power of these four elements to attract the things you desire and banish what no longer serves you. It's also possible to add more elements to the candles you're using in your spells, like crystals (from the earth), herbs (also from the earth), and other components to make your spells more potent.

The great thing about candle magick, also known as sympathetic magic, is that it is simple in nature. For the most part, all you need is a candle. Yes, you need to charge the candle with your intention first, and you can make more intricate spells using other elements, but at the core of this kind of magick is a candle. Some scholars believe that successful candle magick consists of three elements: a clear intention in your head, visualizing your goal and the end result, and focusing on that intention until you can manifest the goal in real life.

Candles and Transformation in Wicca

Wicca is a modern practice of witchcraft, and it incorporates several ancient pagan practices dating back centuries ago. One practice uses candles for spells and as a means of divination or seeking insight and knowledge of the future. Why then do

Wiccans and witches in general use magic, and why has fire been this important for many ancient civilizations? The importance of candle magic is how it uses fire to effect change and manifest desires. Fire is one of the most powerful elements in nature. It possesses the ability to destroy and transform, a beginning and an end of life. A fire can resemble the end of a forest, but it can also lay the foundation for an even more beautiful and greener one. Fire changes everything and anything it touches, a fearsome and powerful transformative power that can be used to transform your own life.

This transformative nature of fire is why it was held in high regard across different cultures and belief systems and why Wiccans harness its power through candle magick. By using candles in our rituals, we bring about change. We end the things that harm us and begin attracting what can help and please us. Wiccans believe that fire can connect us to our true selves, and in that connection lies the power to transform our fate and bring about positive change into our lives. I will show you how you can harness the power of the fire in candle rituals in the upcoming sections.

Candle Color Meaning

Not all candles are alike. Each color corresponds to a different intention, and if you want to make the most of your spell, you need to understand this color code and what each colored candle has the power to attract. Wiccans believe that burning a candle establishes a connection between the physical and spiritual realms using each candle's energy according to its color. It's this color energy that we tap into when we burn candles.

- **Green:** abundance, money, wealth, and fertility.

- **Red:** Courage, lust, love, strength, and sexuality.

- **Pink**: Friendship, love, kindness, and affection.

- **Orange**: Encouragement, attraction, support, and joy.

- **Dark Blue:** Emotional healing, change, adaptability, and psychic powers.

- **Gold:** Connection to the sun, professional success, and money.

- **Yellow:** Protection, divination, wisdom, mental prowess, prosperity, and persuasion.

- **Light Blue**: Patience, health, happiness, and compassion.

- **Brown:** Animal guidance, physical healing, and home.

- **Black:** Banishing negative energies and forces, healing, and psychic protection.

- **Purple:** Power, ambition, female confidence, and stress relief.

- **Gray**: Neutrality

- **Silver:** Connections to the moon, intuition, and reflection

- **White**: Peace, purity and purification, truth, and chastity

One very important note to keep in mind is that white is considered a valid substitute for any candle color. So, if you can't find the colored candle corresponding to your intentions, you can use a white one instead.

Choosing a Candle

There are other elements to consider when selecting a candle besides the color. The size of the candle is something else that you have to keep in mind, despite what some witches will tell you. Many spells require letting your candle burn out entirely, which means selecting one that would take four days to burn isn't exactly ideal. In this case, taper or votive candles are the best as they won't take forever to burn. However, you should also know that some spells require specific types of candles like figure or seven-day candles. In that case, look for those in local stores or online.

When preparing for a spell, never use a candle you've used for another ritual or as a light source in the bathroom or when the power goes out. You should always select new candles for your spells, not a used one that might have picked up energy from the previous usage. Another question that might pop into your head is whether you should use a scented candle. Most Wiccans prefer non-scented candles to avoid distraction.

Preparing the Candles: Cleansing and Charging

According to Wiccan tradition, you cannot buy a candle and immediately use it in a spell. It needs to be cleansed and charged first. There are different cleansing rituals and techniques, and if you have your own, that's fine. To cleanse a candle, you can rub it with sea salt or alcohol. You can also pass the candle through the smoke of sage or incense while focusing on the intention of purifying the candle in preparation for a ritual.

The next step toward preparing the candle is to anoint it, which means dressing it with oil to establish a psychic connection between you and the candle. You'd be charging the candle with your energy and intention meant for the spell so you can prepare it to burn. You can use any natural oil, but many witches go with grapeseed oil since it is odorless. You can select other essential oils with different healing qualities and correspond to certain intentions. For example, if you are about to cast a spell to banish anxiety and stress, you can use lavender oil since lavender is known to be a soother and a powerful tool to get rid of fear and anxiety.

Rub your oil, starting with the top of the candle to the middle. Then begin again from the bottom until the two layers of oil meet at the center. Some Wiccan traditions start from the middle and work the oil to the top and bottom. Some spells will require the addition of natural herbs to the spell. In that case, you can cover the anointed candle in the herbs by rolling it in the mixture you've combined. Alternatively, you can place each herb on the candle's body. Some witches charge their candle by carving a symbol or their intention onto it. This also imbues the candle with the intention of the spell but must be done before dressing it with oil.

Your Intentions Make the Spell

The most important part of candle magick is you, or rather your intentions. We mentioned earlier that you have to be clear with your intention, and I'll add "specific" as well. The clearer you are with your intentions, the more possible it is to attract that wish. You also need to be realistic with your intention and wish for something that can actually happen. For example, you can attract wealth, but wishing for something like being an astronaut and going to space is significantly less likely to happen.

I also recommend summarizing your goal in a single thought or one sentence rather than uttering a monologue or thinking about the whole scenario. If you wish to have a home, just think or say that, but don't go into the details of the house's location and the color of the fence or what kind of dog you wish to have. Before we move on from intentions, I cannot over-stress the importance of not blowing your candles. You want to snuff the candle with your finger or a dedicated tool if you can't leave it to burn out, for example, if you need to go out. If you blow the candle, you're blowing away your intentions, so let's avoid that unless you're banishing something.

By now, you understand what type of candle you need for the goal you have in mind. With your intentions clear, specific, and concise, and the candle cleansed and charged, you can begin your ritual, as I'll show you in the upcoming chapters. Whether it is love or protection, preparing your candle is the first step of the ritual.

Chapter 2: Candle Love Magick

"Your task is not to seek love, but merely to seek and find all the barriers within yourself that you have built against it." – Rumi

This quote is the basis on which positive love magick is based. Love spells are some of the most common in Wicca and other witchcraft movements. However, there are two types of spells to perform to attract love. The first, and the one we'll focus on, is practiced by white witches, and it doesn't change the way a person feels about you or manipulate them into falling for you. It highlights your positive qualities and helps you find the confidence to attract the kind of love you want. The other type is manipulative love spells, which aim to manipulate someone into loving you, which isn't healthy and a practice that should be avoided.

Simple Spell to Attract Love

You'll need a piece of paper and a pen, dried rose petals, cinnamon, honey, a fireproof bowl, a seven-day white candle or any white candle, and a lighter for this spell. Begin this ritual by preparing your magical space, whether that's decluttering or cleansing with sage or incense. You then need to raise the positive energy within you, so do something that makes you feel good. You can put on some soothing music, dance, sing, drum, or simply go for a walk. Anoint your candle with the oil of your choice while focusing on your intentions, thus charging it.

The next step of this spell is to write down this intention on a piece of paper. Make sure you are clear and specific with your intention, which is to attract love for this spell. Fold the piece of paper into squares and make sure it's flat enough to be placed under the candle. Meditate on your intentions for a while. Put the rose petals on top of the candle with a pinch of cinnamon and a couple of teaspoons of honey. Make sure to keep them away from the wick.

Fill the bowl with water but just enough to cover the base of the candle, don't soak it. Put the piece of paper with your intentions under that bowl, and then place the candle in the water and light it. Place the bowl with the candle in it on your altar. Invoke your deities, higher self, ancestors, or whatever spirit guides you wish to bless your ritual and guide you. Ask them to help you attract love.

Meditate on your intention as the candle burns, and visualize yourself finding love and enjoying that feeling of being loved. Conjure a mental image of you attracting affection and no longer craving love because you are satisfied and fulfilled on that emotional level. Let the candle burn out completely — or snuff it out if you have to go, but light it again when you return. When the candle has burned out completely, thank it and throw it away. Carry the piece of paper with your intentions in your wallet or hang it on your fridge.

Spell to Attract Ideal Partner

This is another candle magick spell to help create an attraction between you and someone you like. It happens quite often that we find ourselves attracted to someone that would make an ideal partner, but they might not notice you or don't necessarily think of you in the same way. This candle magick spell acts as a medium between you, helps your romantic interest see you in a different light, and highlights your qualities as a lover.

You need a pink or red candle for this spell, a red pen, white paper, and clear space for this spell. Make sure there are no distractions in your magical space. Set the mood by dimming the lights and maybe playing some soothing music. Sit before your altar and ground yourself. Take three deep breaths and focus on your breathing to calm your mind. Channel your energy into focusing on your romantic interest and how you desire to be with them. Visualize this happening and how you two would be happy together.

Light the red candle and place it on your altar. Grab the red pen and write your first name and your romantic interest's last name on the white paper. Without lifting the pen of the paper, draw two circles around both names while still focusing your intention on being together with this person. Keep visualizing the two of you ending up together. As you do that, repeat this prayer:

May our fates be intertwined

And our love forever defined

We are one

It is done

So, mote it be

Let the candle burn out completely, and don't blow it out. Repeat this spell for seven days in a row, and I'd recommend starting on Friday, the day of the goddess of love, Venus.

Commitment Spell

Sometimes, we find ourselves in good relationships, but they lack commitment. You can be in love with your partner, but they still have a hard time committing to you. This spell can help you strengthen your bond and give your partner the push they need to commit to the relationship fully. This is a full moon spell that aims to add more loyalty and enhance the longevity of your relationship. It's a powerful candle spell that can strengthen your ties with your partner and bind you two together.

You need a long blue or red string, two poppets to represent you and your partner, and two candles. One of them has to be red, and the other can be red or pink. While you can use clay or cloths to make the poppets, you should make it out of the wax of the red or pink candle for this full moon commitment spell. So, melt the candle and make two poppets out of its wax.

Put the red candle between the two wax poppets and wrap the three together with your string to begin the spell. Ensure the knot is tight and the candle is firmly lodged between both poppets, but don't leave a good portion of the string hanging free. When it's a full moon, light the candle and focus on your intentions of having a committed and strengthened relationship. Wrap the hanging part of the string around the poppets and the candle one more time and repeat this prayer:

We are bound together

71

Committed, loving, bound

And so, it shall be

Let the candle burn for a while, and then snuff it out. Light the candle again every night for three days in a row, and on the third night, let it burn completely. Keep the remaining wax from this spell, and don't get rid of it. You can keep a healthy, committed relationship as long as you keep this wax safe.

Honey Jar Love Spell

The use of honey in spells dates back to ancient civilizations. Witches have used it for a long with love rituals, and when paired with candle magick, you can create a very powerful spell. The great thing about honey jar love spells is how diverse they are. You can use this spell to attract love, ignite a spark between you and a certain person, or rekindle the flame with an ex or an old crush. It doesn't even have to be a romantic relationship. You may want to mend a relationship with a friend or a relative and use a honey jar spell for that intention. Adding a candle to a honey jar gives you options with the spell, as I'll show you now.

Begin by writing the name of the person you wish to attract or fix a relationship with — write it three times. Then, turn the paper by a 90-degree angle and write yours down three times as well so that the letters of both names overlap. Draw a circle around both names, and within that circle, you're going to write your intention. The most important part is not to lift your pen while writing all this down. The next part is where you focus on your intention, and it's crucial for the success of this spell. Whether you want to reconcile with a loved one or ignite a flame of love, just focus on your intentions, and visualize the outcome coming to fruition. You can add the dots and cross the t's when you're done circling the names and the intentions.

Fold this paper with the names and the intention to fit inside the honey jar. Put the piece of paper inside the jar and let your fingers touch the honey. When you remove your fingers, say this prayer:

As sweet as this honey is, so shall my connection with ___ be.

When you say the prayer, lick your fingers and close the jar. Then, you will use candle magick to set your intentions onto the universe and transform your relationship with this person. You need to select a candle beforehand suited for your intentions. Choose red if you want someone to fall for you or if you want to strengthen a bond between you and your partner, or pink if you want to highlight the nonromantic love between you and someone. You could also just use a white candle as it is neutral and can be used with any intention.

Place the candle on top of the honey jar with the folded paper and light it. Let this candle burn down until it's finished, and focus on your intentions as it does. Meditate and visualize this honey jar candle spell attracting the love and happiness you deserve. When the candle is burned out completely, don't discard it but store it in a place that only you know. After seven full days, repeat this ritual, and keep doing it on the same day, once every week, until your intentions come to fruition.

Candle Magick to Banish a Toxic Ex

This spell is a bit different from the previous few. It's not to attract love but to move from it. People can easily find themselves trapped in a toxic relationship with an abusive partner, and moving on from your feelings toward them is never easy. This powerful candle ritual will help you banish a toxic ex from your life and move on.

You need a black candle, a fireproof bowl, white sage, Florida water, scissors, and black cotton threads or yarn (prepare several yards). Start the ritual by cleansing your magical space of any lingering negative energy. Open the windows and light some incense or sage. Spray some Florida water in the corners of your room to create a safe and sacred circle. Sit before your altar and ground yourself. You can meditate to clear your thoughts. When you feel ready, light the candle, and focus on your intentions of banishing this toxic ex from your life. Visualize yourself free of loving them and no longer held back by those feelings. Focus on this intention while setting your gaze on the black candle.

Bind your feet together with the thread and say this:

This thread is holding me back and stopping me from moving forward.

Next, tie your hands together and say:

These bonds are stopping me from receiving love.

Meditate again and focus on the negative experience you've had with this ex and how you wish to be free of it. Let the threads around your hands and feet absorb this energy. When you're ready, cut the threads with the scissors and be careful not to harm yourself. As you cut the threads laced with negativity, say:

I banish ___ from my life, and I release my ties to them.

I am whole again, and I shall move forward.

Burn the threads in the flame of the black candle, and toss them in the fireproof bowl. Get rid of the ashes of the threads and bury them in the ground somewhere far from your home. Let the candle burn down completely and visualize the healthier and happier version of yourself with that ex no longer part of your life.

Whether you wish to attract love or banish a toxic relationship, these candle spells can help you manifest that intention. You just need to believe that these rituals will work and let yourself be filled with positive energy to make them work. As you can see from this section, candle magick can be very powerful if paired with rituals and other practices, and you can use it to attract love and even heal from physical and emotional pain, as you'll see in this upcoming chapter.

Chapter 3: Candle Magic Spells for Healing

"The wound is the place where the Light enters you." — Rumi

Sometimes, toxic relationships and feelings of loneliness from not having love in our lives can leave us emotionally scarred. Some relationships can even leave you physically scared. This is why I've chosen to add candle spells to help you heal from these wounds. What's worse is not knowing what ails you. In a few cases, doctors can't find the answer and are flabbergasted about why you are in pain. We'll also explore some spells to help treat unknown pains. Remember, however, that these spells are not a substitute for seeking medical care. They can, however, complement the remedies given to you by doctors.

Pain Healing Spell

This ritual should be performed over two days, Saturday and Sunday, or entirely on a Sunday. It's a healing spell to help you regenerate from an emotional or physical injury. There are no specific ingredients for this spell. You can include herbs, natural crystals/stones, and essential oils that have a soothing effect on you and are blessed with regenerative qualities. However, you will need a candle corresponding to your intention: dark blue for emotional healing, brown for physical healing, or white.

Begin this ritual by casting your magical circle. You need to create a space where you are safe and can heal. You can make the circle out of natural stones with healing properties like quartz or amethyst. You can also make an invisible circle using an athame or your finger. Make the circle in a clockwise direction, with you in it, and visualize that it is made of protective light that can shield and heal you.

The first part of this ritual is about releasing what pains you. This means that you first need to acknowledge the injury or the trauma that left you emotionally or physically scarred. You can journal about it or focus on what happened so you can move on. Write down whatever happened that left you in need of healing. Breathe in and out slowly as you think about what happened. Then, rip the pages out of your journal and shred them. Imagine that the pain is leaving your body, and the tension is fading as you do so.

Anoint the candle with essential oils and herbs that have a special place in your heart, then light it. Light the candle and focus on its flame. Let its healing light wash over you and fill you with light that will heal your scars. Take in that healing energy coming from the candle and meditate on your intention. Conjure a mental image of a healthier you that is no longer suffering from the pain of a past injury or trauma. Let that light wrap around every fiber of your being and replace the negative energy you have released earlier onto the paper. As you focus on the flame of the candle, say this prayer:

By the light of this candle

My wounds will heal

This healing flame will wash away my pain

And it shall never return again

So, mote it be

Perform this spell once every week until the candle is spent.

Healing Disease Ritual

This particular ritual is very important right now, as the world faces a global pandemic. It offers healing and protection for you and your loved ones from disease and sickness. Prepare your magical space as you normally would and cleanse the room first with sage or incense. Charge the magical space with the intention of healing from sickness and pain.

You need three candles, green, blue, and white, and a holder for each. You'll need an essential oil to anoint your candles or a mixture. You can make a mixture of rosemary, lavender, eucalyptus, and cedarwood oils, all powerful elements with healing and protective qualities. Prepare an athame or a pin, a piece of paper or a leaf from the earth, and a pen. If you can find gold ink, that'd be great. If not, use any pen.

To start the ritual, cast your magical circle and invoke whichever deities you ask for guidance during your rituals. Raise your energy by chanting or dancing. Take deep breaths to calm and center yourself if you want. Whatever you usually do to prepare for spells, do it. When you feel ready, use the pin or athame to carve the word 'protect' on the white candle, or you can carve a symbol associated with healing for you. Anoint the candle with the essential oil mixture and/or any herbs you associate with protection. Hold it in your hand and visualize a white light spreading out of the candle, engulfing and shielding you, your home, and your loved ones from pain and sickness. Light the candle and say a protective chant:

By the flames of this candle, I am protected.

I am safe from illness and disease.

This white light shields my loved ones and me.

So, mote it be.

Then, carve 'heal' on the blue candle and anoint it with essential oils and herbs you associate with healing or the same mixture you used with the one above. Hold the candle in your hand and visualize it glowing in a blue light that will grow and engulf you. It will heal your body and that of loved ones and remove any sickness. Let that soothing and restorative energy fill you up. Light the blue candle and say:

By the flames of this blue candle, I am healed.

This healing light surrounds us and grants us recovery and good health.

We are whole; we are healed; we are healthy. So, mote it be.

This last part of the spell prevents the sickness from returning to your body or someone you care about. Grab the green candle and carve "security" on it. Anoint it with oils and place healing herbs on it. Hold the candle and visualize a green light spreading out of it to engulf you and your house with everyone in it. This green light is a security blanket, keeping you and your loved ones safe and securing you from ever contracting that sickness again. Light the candle and say:

By the flames of this green candle, the disease is gone and shall never return.

We are secured, prospering, and comforted, and so it shall be.

Write down these intentions for protection, healing, and security on the piece of paper. Fold it twice and seal it with some melted wax from the white candle. Keep this paper on your altar or by your bed to keep your intentions of health and security alive. Let the three candles burn out over three days.

Spell to Banish Depression

This candle healing spell is used to banish depression, anxiety, or other mental/emotional ailments. With the power of your intentions, you will charge ritual candles with your energy and desire to heal from depression. As always, remember that this spell is not a substitute for seeking medical help.

You need a blue candle for this spell, an athame/pin, incense, a piece of paper and a pen, a healing crystal (selenite), essential oils, and some healing herbs like rosemary and lavender. Prepare for the ritual by cleansing your magical space and then casting your circle. Sit before your altar and center yourself. Begin by carving your intention on the blue candle using the athame or pin. Be specific about what you wish to heal and release, and focus on that intention in your head. You can write something along the lines of "Banish depression" or "Become happier and banish anxiety."

Next, anoint the candle with essential oils of your choosing — go for essential oils with healing properties like sandalwood, eucalyptus, and peppermint. Charge this candle with your intention of banishing depression and becoming free of its shackles. Keep focusing on your intention as you anoint the candle, and then add the herbs. Roll it in a mixture of rosemary, lavender, garden sage, and peppermint that you've grounded earlier. The herbs will stick to the candle now that it has been anointed with the oil.

After consecrating the candle, grab the pen and paper and write down your intention on it. You can write your name as well. It's something like this: *I __ thus banish depression and anxiety from my life.* When you're done writing what you wish to banish, fold the paper, and put it on the altar. Place your blue candle over it. Grab the selenite crystal and visualize it absorbing the negativity from your body. Channel all the negative thoughts and bad feelings you've ever had into the stone and let it drain your body of the fear and the sadness.

Holding the crystal in one hand, light the blue candle with the other. Focus on the candle's flame and imagine that your depression is fading away just like the candle's smoke. Keep meditating on your intention as the candle burns, with the healing crystal in your hand, until the candle burns out completely.

Using these spells, you can invoke the help of your ancestors or deities and the universe to heal from emotional and physical pain. Don't cast these spells if you're in a bad headspace, and make sure you are filled with positive energy as you perform these healing rituals. After learning how to cast a candle healing spell, I will show you how to cast protection spells in this upcoming chapter. Peace of mind and enlightenment can be achieved, but they must be protected from the darkness surrounding us.

Chapter 4: Candle Magic Spells for Protection

"Goodness is sparked by a caution for the sake of what is good, not a fear of what is bad." – Criss Jami

Witchcraft does not preach fear. It doesn't tell us to always be on guard of the evil forces at work around us and the negative energies we have to be mindful of. Witchcraft does, however, preach protecting what you love. There is much good in your life, even if you don't always see it. This is why it is your responsibility as a witch with the power to take action to protect that good. These spells I will outline will help you protect yourself, your household, and your loved ones from any darkness that may seek to harm them.

Simple Protection Spell

This spell is simple, and any witch can cast it to protect her physical and spiritual self. You need a black candle, black salt, white sage, star anise, protective crystals like black tourmaline or amethyst, a fireproof bowl, rosemary, essential oils, and mortar & pestle. Cleanse your magical space using sage or incense, or however you usually do it. I'd recommend using the black salt to cast your circle for this spell as, within it, you'd be safe from any negative energy or ill intentions. You can also place four protective crystals in each quarter of your circle to amplify its protection.

Begin heating your essential oils in the fireproof bowl or a diffuser if you have one. Place the oil inside your circle and start mixing your herbs together. Use the mortar & pestle to mix the star anise, rosemary, and white sage. Add this herbal mixture to the oil and focus on your intention. Visualize yourself being shielded from any harm that may befall you or your loved ones. Light the black candle on your altar and set your gaze on its flame while still focusing on that intention to summon a protective shield. As you do that, repeat this chant:

By the flame of this black candle

And the power of these herbs and oils and crystals

I ask for protection from all harm

That may befall me or my own

May the goddess shield me and help me remain strong

I am safe from negativity and everything that is wrong

So, mote it be

Let the candle burn out completely while meditating and focusing on your protection. You can keep one or two of the crystals with you as a symbol of the protection you're not blessed with.

Home Protection Spell

Some practices are dedicated to protecting your home, like hanging protective herbs or crystals or an iron horseshoe to prevent negative energies and ill intentions from entering your space. This spell is a more potent approach to protect your home from negative vibrations and energies that might seep through to your home and affect everyone in it.

You need a small black candle, an athame or pin, dried sage (or sage oil), a rosemary stick (rosemary oil is fine, too), and two fireproof bowls. Cleanse your tools and your home before you begin this ritual. Take the black candle and carve a protective symbol or sigil on it using the athame or pin. Protective symbols include the Eye of Horus, Solar Cross, Hamsa, Triquetra, and the Bindrune. Look each of those up if you're unsure of how to draw them. If you're using oils instead of dried herbs, anoint the candle with them. If not, place the herbs on the candle, but leave some aside.

This ritual requires that you sit before your front door, so you can temporarily move your altar there for this spell. If that space is not available, you can perform it anywhere. Put both fireproof bowls in front of you with the candle in one. Place the protective herbs in the other bowl. You can use two candles in this spell; if that is the case, you'll put an anointed candle in each bowl. Calm your mind and breathe in and out slowly, focusing on your breathing. Whether it's a candle or herbal mixture or two candles, light whatever is in both bowls.

Let the scent of the anointed candles or the herbal mixture burn and fill your house with cleansing and protective energy. Focus on the candle's flame and let it fill you with positive energy, replacing any lingering negative thoughts you might have carried into your home. Like fire transforms all, so will the flames of the candle transform any negative energy in your home into love and peace. In this focused, meditative state of mind, repeat this chant:

I call on rosemary and sage to impart protection upon my abode and those in it

Protect and cleanse my home

May the candle flame transform negativity into pure energy

And ill intentions toward me into love and light and joy

So, mote it be

When you feel ready, open your front door, release the smoke of the candle and/or herbs, and visualize it carrying any negative energy along. Let the candle burn down completely. You can carry them and walk around the house to cleanse every room and then bury their remains far from your home.

Protection Spell Against Negative and Hateful People

This spell is a bit more specific as it aims to block any negative energy coming your way from harmful people. It can shield you from their ill intentions and ward off any curses or hate coming your way. For this spell, the ingredients you need are seven needles, a small bottle with a cork, rosemary, and a black candle.

As always, cleanse the room and the tools you'll use before beginning. Then, place the rosemary in the bottle while focusing your intention on blocking negative energy and hatred from affecting you and the people you care about. Visualize this destructive energy being channeled into the needles, after which the rosemary will contain it. Light the black candle and focus on its flame that acts as a powerful shield against hatred and negativity.

Start adding the needles one by one into the small bottle, and as you do that, say aloud what each needle represents. The needles are hatred, negativity, hexes, curses, jealousy, and other ill intentions that may be aimed at you. With seven needles and seven intentions placed in the bottle, seal it with the cork. The rosemary will work to neutralize these negative energies and bad intentions, and the black candle will banish them. Tilt the black candle and use some of its wax to seal the cork even further. Bury the bottle somewhere far from your home, and let the banishing candle burn out completely.

Spell to Ward Off an Attack

Witches have a highly developed intuition and can often sense if and when someone cast a curse or hex on them. This candle spell is ideal for warding off such attacks. It will reverse the spell on the attacker and protect you and your loved ones. Smudge your altar and your magical items and perform a cleansing ritual on yourself to release any negative energy.

You need a small mirror that you don't need; it can be a hand mirror or any other portable one. On the window next to your bed, put the mirror with its front facing the sky. You will need to charge this mirror with your intention to reverse the curse and ward off the attack. Light a black candle to begin the ritual. Repeat this chant as you focus your gaze on the flame:

By the light of this black candle, I banish the curse that was put on me and my loved ones.

This mirror shall reverse the spell, and the negative energy that was meant for me shall be turned on the attacker.

Channel all your energy to the mirror and the candle. The candle will act as a shield to protect you from negative energy and banish evil intentions, while the mirror will reverse any harmful spell that might have been cast with you as the target. Visualize the hex or the curse and negative energy meant for you bouncing off the mirror toward the person who targeted you. Sit by the window and let the candle burn out as you meditate on your intention.

These candle spells can provide you with protection against the negative energy we encounter daily. You might not think that it affects you, but it does. Negative energy seeping into your home can affect your relationships with your loved ones as well as your peace of mind, so you need this kind of protection. Next, we will discuss how to invite abundance into your life now that you're in a good place physically, mentally, and spiritually.

Chapter 5: Candle Magic Spells for Abundance

"When you are grateful, fear disappears, and abundance appears." — Anthony Robbins

Gratitude brings more abundance into your life, but practicing gratitude isn't always easy. It's a bit of a dilemma for many people as they can't practice gratitude without abundance, and they can't attract abundance without being grateful. This is where candle magick comes in. I will show you some spells to embrace the good fortune in your life and attract more abundance and joy.

Spell to Attract Abundance

Contrary to popular belief, abundance isn't just money. Abundance is happiness and wealth and the richness that can only fill your life if you're truly grateful. This candle spell can bring you luck, happiness, wealth, gratitude, and much more. I recommend doing this ritual for several days or weeks in a row, starting on the new moon, which marks new beginnings and attracts good fortune.

Make sure your magical space is cleansed and that you're comfortable and in a good mood. Whatever you usually do to charge yourself with positive energy, do it. Dance, sing, drum, play music, take a ritual bath, read, or just put on your favorite outfit. Prepare a green candle for this ritual and place a crystal for abundance on your altar like citrine. When you feel ready, grounded, and calm, sit before your altar and hold the candle in your hand. Meditate on the things you have in your life that you're grateful for. It doesn't have to be something as significant as wealth or marriage. It can be something you did to help someone or a hobby you have. There are always things to be grateful for, and you need to think about those for a while.

Abundance is gratitude for the things you are blessed with, and it's also attracting more. You need that balance, and you have to visualize it in your head because without gratitude and the desire to attract more, you can't attract abundance. Light the candle and place it on your altar. Then, declare your intentions aloud. What kind of abundance do you wish to attract? Is it wealth? Gratitude? Joy? How would that feel, and why do you want it? Don't hold back and ask the universe for your heart's deepest desires, and release this positive energy into the candle. Picture these positive wishes fueling the candle's flame and whisper it all to the fire. Make sure you're close to the candle but be careful not to get burned.

After speaking your intentions, close your eyes, meditate on these wishes and let yourself fill with positive energy. Let the candle burn, and grab your journal. Write down what abundance means in your life and why you wish to attract it, or write personal affirmations. This is one of those few rituals where you should blow the candle to release your intentions into the universe. Take the citrine stone off your altar and carry it in your pocket.

Spell to Attract Prosperity and Abundance

This is another prosperity and abundance spell that can be used to attract wealth and money or whatever you wish to be abundant in your life. You need a small green candle, a coin, fireproof bowl, an athame or pin, square green cloth, pure vanilla or vanilla bean, and powdered cinnamon or pure Ceylon cinnamon oil. This spell should be performed on a waxing moon to charge it with lunar power and attract abundance.

Carve a prosperity symbol on the green candle with the pin or athame like the number '3,' which corresponds to abundance and good fortune. You can also write down words like wealth, joy, abundance, or prosperity instead. Consecrate the candle with the cinnamon and vanilla, and recite this prayer: *I call on these magic herbs to unleash my potential. May they attract prosperity and good fortune into my life. Money, joy, and abundance come to me, so mote it be.*

Place the coin in the fireproof bowl and the candle on top of it. Light the candle and focus on your intentions. Visualize yourself turning around and prosperity filling it. Let these positive feelings wash over you. Let the green candle burn down entirely, then take the coin from underneath the wax and wrap it in the green cloth. Carry it in your wallet or your pocket wherever you go. Get rid of any remaining wax far from your home; bury it if you can.

Spell to Attract Money

While the spells above were for abundance and could implicitly include money, this one is specifically for attracting money. It's a simple ritual to bring more money into your life. You could add more ingredients if you wish, but you only need a green candle to try this spell out. You don't need to be in debt to perform this ritual, as its purpose is to attract wealth regardless of your current financials.

To cast this spell, you need to raise your energy more than you usually do at the beginning of a ritual. So, perform an energetic activity like chanting, dancing, or drumming. Make some noise and create positive energy within you. Sit before your altar and consecrate the candle when you feel comfortable and positive enough. Use essential oils and/or herbs you feel comfortable with and are associated with abundance like rosemary, basil, dandelion, and calendula. Carve your name on the candle using a pin or athame.

Light the candle and place it on the altar. Stare into the flame and let your mind drift away into a deep meditative state. Close your eyes and begin to visualize money flowing into your life, and you buy all the things you want with it. Let that positive feeling of wealth fill you up, and make sure the money and the things you'll do with it are real in your head. As you visualize this, repeat this prayer three times:

Wealth, money, and fortune flow into my life

In no means that harm or pain another

Fill my life with joy and prosperity

May wealth find me in perpetuity

So, mote it be

Light the green candle every day while repeating this chant three times every night until it burns out. Don't throw it away. Retain it and wait for the money to flow into your life as you have wished for.

Chapter 6: Candle Magic Spells for Employment

"Joblessness is a time for reflection" — Sunday Adelaja

Everyone struggles with their professional lives at some point, but that is no reason to despair. With enough luck and hard work and these spells, you can attract any job, even your dream one. Cast these spells when you are facing trouble on the job front, whether you've been unemployed for a while or stuck in a hopeless job that you don't like.

Spell for Good Luck with Job Hunting

Candle magick is very powerful and effective for those looking for help with employment in general. You can change the color of the candle depending on the purpose of your spell. For this one, you want confidence and good fortune while you're job hunting, so get a yellow or gold candle. You'll also need olive oil and matches or a lighter.

Put the candle on the altar and make sure you've prepared the space for the spell. Anoint it with olive oil or use other essential oils that have a special meaning for you. Charge the candle with your intentions, and make sure you transfer only positive energy into it. Light the gold or yellow candle and repeat this prayer three times:

For me, a good job awaits

By the blessing of this bright light

And the power of this flame

There is a place for me

And a good job awaits me

I have faith that the universe will help me

So, mote it be

Repeat this three times, and let the candle burn for nine minutes while focusing on your intention and visualizing yourself getting a job offer. Draw a mental image of yourself enjoying your new job and finding good fortune on the employment front. Then, snuff out the flame and repeat this ritual once every Sunday until you get that job offer you've been waiting for or the candle is spent. If by then you haven't received the job offer, get a new candle, and repeat the ritual every Sunday until you do.

Career Success Spell

Sometimes, it's about keeping and protecting your job rather than finding one, and this spell helps you do that. This ritual can give you a much-needed boost in your professional life. You'll need some essential oils: rosemary, cinnamon, and ginger, four candles; white, green, red, and yellow, and a candle snuff. Prepare a piece of paper and a pen.

Cleanse your energy however you usually do, but I'd recommend taking a ritual bath with some rosemary oil or leaves. When you feel refreshed and ready, go to your altar, and write down what you wish to attract to your career. It can be protecting your job or getting a promotion or a raise. Try to be specific about your intentions and write down what kind of career success you hope to attract. Let the intentions flow out of you and into the paper.

Next, anoint each candle with a drop of each of the essential oils you've prepared. Ginger will attract good fortune and bless your career, cinnamon will attract money, and rosemary will banish negative energy and misfortune as well as any blockages that might be stopping you from manifesting your goals. Place the four candles around the piece of paper with your intentions and light them. The green candle will attract wealth and abundance, the white one will dispel negative energy, the red candle will give you courage and power to accomplish your goals, and the yellow one will boost your confidence and help you achieve your goals.

With the four candles lit, close your eyes and relax. Sink into a deep meditative state where you can visualize these intentions coming to life. Picture a more successful and accomplished version of yourself and take control of your destiny. Meditate for a few minutes and repeat a chant:

By the power of these candles, I ask for guidance and aid.

May the universe bless my career, and these flames bring me fortune and good luck.

Snuff out your candles and repeat this candle ritual for six days in a row, and on the seventh day, let each candle burn out completely. Keep the paper with your intentions and aspirations with you until you achieve what was written in it. Once you do, burn the paper, and thank the universe for manifesting your goals.

Conclusion

"No one saves us but ourselves. No one can, and no one may. We ourselves must walk the path."— Gautama Buddha

In this book, I set out to show you how you can take control of your destiny. Sooner or later, we all experience some misfortune in life, but it's up to us to pick ourselves up and move on. It's up to you to surrender to the hardships of life or to take action and seize control of your destiny. Using these spells, you can attract the things you've often dreamed of and think impossible. You can also banish the negative feelings and darkness that seek to hold you back and stop you from realizing your full potential.

Candle magick is powerful magick, but it's only as powerful as you believe it to be. With enough positive energy and faith, you can manifest these dreams of yours. You can heal from past trauma and injury. You can find love and be emotionally satisfied. You can protect your house and everyone in it. You can find the job you've dreamed of for many years. With candle spells, you can fill your life with an abundance of joy and satisfaction. I added spells that are easy to apply and require minimal ingredients. The beauty of candle magick is that you can practice it and change your reality with only a candle and your own energy. You just need to start, and the spells in this book are a great place to do that. So, read these spells, find yourself some candles, and make things happen.

Finally, I hope that you enjoy this book as much as I enjoyed writing it. If you did, it would be wonderful if you could take a short minute and leave a review on Amazon, as your kind feedback is much appreciated and so very important. Thank you.

References

A candle healing spell. (2021, November 2).   Well Divined. https://welldivined.com/a-candle-healing-spell/

A protection spell against negative people. (2021, November 2). Well Divined. https://welldivined.com/a-protection-spell-against-negative-people/

A simple protection spell. (2021, November 2).   Well Divined. https://welldivined.com/a-simple-protection-spell/

A witch's guide to cord-cutting, the simple ritual to get over your ex. (n.d.). Vice.Com. Retrieved from https://www.vice.com/en/article/mbz3na/how-to-do-cord-cutting-ritual-witch-spell-breakup

All Answers Ltd. (2021, December 31). History of candle magic. Ukessays.Com; UK Essays. https://www.ukessays.com/essays/cultural-studies/the-history-of-candle-magick-cultural-studies-essay.php

An astrological forecast for 2022. (2021, December 30). Goop. https://goop.com/ca-en/wellness/spirituality/horoscope-predictions-2022/

Best Love Spells - Improve your relationships & experiences with others. (2021, August 13). Baltimore Magazine. https://www.baltimoremagazine.com/special/best-love-spells-improve-your-relationships-and-experiences-with-others/

Candle magic for beginners. (2017, June 29). Wiccan Spells. https://wiccanspells.info/wiccan-pagan-articles/candle-magic-for-beginners/

Comiskey, B. (2019a, March 7). Abundance spell. Tip of the Moon. https://tipofthemoon.store/spells/abundance

Comiskey, B. (2019b, June 4). Healing spell. Tip of the Moon. https://tipofthemoon.store/spells/healing-spell

Dombrowski, K. (2020, March 17). Blessing spell for protection, healing, and security in response to Covid-19 —. Kiki Dombrowski. https://www.kikidombrowski.com/blog/blessing-spell-for-protection-healing-and-security-in-response-to-covid-19

Love spells that work, best love spell caster guide. (2021, August 17). Juneau Empire. https://www.juneauempire.com/national-marketplace/love-spells-that-work-best-love-spell-caster-guide/

May, A. (2020, February 7). 9 powerful protection symbols explained. Welcome To Wicca Now. https://wiccanow.com/9-protection-symbols/

Morgan, B. (2018, October 2). You need these magical spell candles. House Beautiful. https://www.housebeautiful.com/shopping/home-accessories/g23572014/magic-spell-candles/

Pollux, A. (2019a, November 21). Our #1 career success spell for attaining your goals. Welcome To Wicca Now. https://wiccanow.com/our-career-success-spell-to-help-attain-your-goals/

Pollux, A. (2019b, November 27). An easy abundance spell using cinnamon and vanilla. Welcome To Wicca Now. https://wiccanow.com/an-easy-abundance-spell-using-cinnamon-and-vanilla/

Pollux, A. (2019c, November 28). Our powerful home protection spell with sage and Rosemary. Welcome To Wicca Now.

https://wiccanow.com/powerful-home-protection-spell-with-sage-and-rosemary/

Smith, E. W. (2019, May 3). A beginner's guide to candle magic. Refinery29.Com; Refinery29. https://www.refinery29.com/en-us/what-is-candle-magic-meaning

The transforming power of fire - Pepi de Boissieu. (n.d.). Pepideboissieu.Com. Retrieved from https://pepideboissieu.com/The-transforming-power-of-fire

Ward, K. (2021, December 23). Your everything-you-need-to-know intro to candle magick. Cosmopolitan. https://www.cosmopolitan.com/lifestyle/a31133533/candle-magic-colors-meaning/

Wigington, P. (n.d.). How to use candle magic in spells. Learn Religions. Retrieved from https://www.learnreligions.com/introduction-to-candle-magic-2561684

Your guide to candle magic. (n.d.). Rylandpeters. Retrieved from https://rylandpeters.com/blogs/health-mind-body-and-spirit/your-guide-to-candle-magic

(N.d.). Lamag.Com. Retrieved from https://www.lamag.com/article/best-love-spells-magical-ways-to-influence-relationships-and-love

The Easy Guide to Wicca for Beginners

By Frank Bawdoe

© Copyright 2022 Frank Bawdoe